Read & Respond

SECTION 1

The Demon Headmaster

SECTION 2

Guided reading

SECTION 3

Shared reading

SECTION 4

Plot, character and setting

SECTION 5

Talk about it

SECTION 6

Get writing

SECTION 7

Assessment

Author: Jillian Powell

Commissioning Editor: Rachel Mackinnon

Development Editor: Marion Archer

Assistant Editor: Rachel Coombs

Series Designer: Anna Oliwa

Designer: Dan Prescott

Illustrations: Mike Lacey (Beehive Illustration)

Designed using Adobe InDesign

Published by Scholastic Ltd,
Book End, Range Road, Witney,
Oxfordshire OX29 0YD
www.scholastic.co.uk

Printed by Bell & Bain
1 2 3 4 5 6 7 8 9 2 3 4 5 6 7 8 9 0 1

British Library Cataloguing-in-Publication Data
A catalogue record for this book is available from the British Library.

ISBN 978-1407-12726-2

Acknowledgements

The publishers gratefully acknowledge permission to reproduce the following copyright material:
Oxford University Press for the use of text extracts and the cover from *The Demon Headmaster* by Gillian Cross. Text © 1982, Gillian Cross. (1982, Oxford University Press).
Every effort has been made to trace copyright holders for the works reproduced in this book, and the publishers apologise for any inadvertent omissions.

The Demon Headmaster

SECTION 1

About the book

The Demon Headmaster is the first in a series of novels by the Carnegie Medal-winning author Gillian Cross. First published in 1982, the novel introduces the main characters in the series, Dinah Glass, an orphan from a children's home who comes to live with the Hunter family, her new 'brothers' Lloyd and Harvey, and the mysterious and sinister Headmaster who runs their school with chilling control. As the story begins, the older brother Lloyd is dreading the invasion of a girl into their family life and suspects Dinah will be 'one of them' at school, not an outsider like themselves. What they are 'outside' is only revealed as the story unfolds.

The novel centres on the evil plans of the Demon Headmaster, a shady character with strange hypnotic powers which he uses to enforce control at the school. Never named, the Headmaster remains an enigmatic figure throughout, reminiscent of a Bond villain with his false charm and sinister plans for world domination. The Hunter boys are among the few children at the school who have resisted hypnotism and formed SPLAT, the Society for the Protection of our Lives Against Them, a secret subversive organisation for the outsiders.

When she starts school, Dinah finds herself succumbing to the Headmaster's mysterious powers, but she eventually uses her will and wit to revolt against 'them' and joins SPLAT in their efforts to foil the Headmaster's plans. The group discover that the Headmaster is planning to hijack a school quiz on the popular TV programme the Eddy Hair Show, to attempt to hypnotise the masses over the airwaves. The children must act fast if they are to stop his evil plan. As the story reaches its climax, Dinah triumphs by outwitting the Headmaster, with the help of Harvey.

About the author

Gillian Cross was born in London on 24 December 1945, the year the Second World War ended. Growing up, she loved reading books and wanted to write stories of her own, inventing her own 'serial' based on the lives of school friends with whom she shared the train journey home from school. After studying at Oxford and Sussex universities, she did a range of jobs, including being an assistant to a Member of Parliament.

Her first novel, *The Runaway*, was published in 1979. She says that her ideas come from people, places or 'scenes' she sees around her, and that she begins a novel by asking questions about the characters, drafting the storyline to discover what happens to them. Married with four grown-up children, she enjoys swimming, gardening, playing the piano and orienteering – exploring and discovering routes, just as she explores and discovers storylines each time she begins a new novel. Gillian has been writing children's books for over 20 years and is a winner of the Carnegie Medal (1990) for her novel *Wolf* and the Smarties Book Prize and Whitbread Children's Novel Award (1992) for *The Great Elephant Chase.*

Facts and figures

First published: 1982

Adapted into a television series by the BBC 1996–98.

To date it is Gillian's best-selling title, with paperback sales into six figures.

Guided reading

SECTION 2

First reading

The first reading should be used to familiarise the children with the story, characters and key themes.

Look together at the front cover of the book. Ask the children what they think the story is about – what do they learn from the title and illustration? (Some children may already have read this or other books in the series, so stress the importance of not spoiling the story for others.) Encourage them to describe the characters' expressions in the picture. How do the children look? (Frightened, wary?) What is the Headmaster's expression? (Angry, threatening?)

Turn to the back cover and read the blurb together. Ask what more they have learned about the story (school setting, key characters, sinister goings-on and his dark plans). Invite the children to pick out adjectives (*threatening, frightened, weird, strange, eerie, dark, spooky, fun*). What type of story do they think this will be? (Realistic, scary, science fiction or adventure?) What is the 'hook' in the blurb that invites us to read the story? (What are the Headmaster's strange powers and dark plans and can the children escape them?)

Chapters 1 to 3

Read the first chapter together and ask the children what is happening. (A girl called Dinah is coming to live with a foster family, the Hunters.) Discuss why Lloyd is so fed up about it. (He hates the idea of a girl in the family.) Read on through Chapters 2 and 3, up to *...a door which had the single word HEADMASTER painted on it.* Ask: *What do we learn about the school?* (Lloyd and Harvey are 'normal' but most of the rest of the children are strange in some way and seem to behave like robots.) Continue reading Chapter 3, pausing at the description of the Headmaster. Invite the children to think of some epithets to describe him (such as, eerie, creepy, cold, sinister). Read to the end of the chapter and consider what questions are left unanswered. (Why has Dinah fallen asleep? Why does she have a prick on her finger?)

Chapters 4 to 5

Read Chapter 4 and talk with the class about what else they have learned about the Headmaster. (He uses his strange green eyes to hypnotise the children.) Ask: *Why is Dinah surprised at what comes out of her mouth about the Headmaster and the school?* (She does not intend to say those words, but they come out mechanically.) Briefly discuss the idea of hypnotism and encourage the children to say what they know about it, including how it is used (for example, for entertainment shows or to stop people smoking). What question still remains unanswered? (What is happening to the children while they are under hypnosis?) Continue reading through Chapter 5 and encourage the children to speculate on what Harvey witnesses in the hall. What might the Headmaster be doing? (Is he brainwashing the children, making them learn scientific facts parrot-fashion or programming them in some way?) Why is Lloyd reluctant to tell Dinah what they know? (He thinks she is one of them, and is a spy who will report back to the Headmaster or the prefects.)

Chapters 6 to 9

Begin reading Chapter 6, pausing after *...slipped it into her head without her knowing.* Ask the children how Dinah might know the scientific facts. (Has she absorbed them while she was being hypnotised in the school hall?) What does this suggest about the Headmaster? (He is force-feeding children facts, or maybe he has some sinister, alien purpose.) Continue reading to the end of Chapter 7 and invite the children to comment on the prefects' punishment of the children (cruel, sadistic, even dangerous). Why does Dinah say this punishment would cause a scandal for the Headmaster? (He is responsible for the care of the children and the authorities would not allow them to be bullied, harmed or have their health put at risk.) Pause at the end of the chapter to ask why Dinah is now covering up what happened. (The Headmaster hypnotised her again when he followed her to the cloakroom.)

Guided reading

SECTION 2

Read on through the next two chapters and encourage the children to explain what Harvey now has to do to avoid further punishment (complete some difficult sums). Ask: *What has Dinah kept hidden and why?* (Dinah is very clever, she has kept it a secret because she does not want to get picked on or bullied.) Pause after *It wasn't me that told...* to ask the children if they can recall who the real telltale was (Jeff). What danger is foreshadowed at the end of Chapter 9? (The Headmaster's ambitions, and what he might do with his brainwashed 'army'.)

Chapters 10 to 12

Read Chapter 10, pausing after *And Mandy helps us with our sums...* to ask the children to explain the acronym SPLAT (The Society for the Protection of our Lives Against Them) and who they are (the children who are not under the Headmaster's powers). Continue reading to the end of Chapter 11 and encourage the children to explain what goes wrong with SPLAT's plan. (The Headmaster discovers the recording device and Dinah is blackmailed into co-operating with his plans in order to protect Harvey.) As you read Chapter 12, ensure the children understand the Headmaster's plan. (To get the children to win the TV quiz so that he can hypnotise the masses over the airwaves.) Finish the chapter and identify the 'hook' that makes us want to read on. (The reader is left wondering how SPLAT can stop the TV crew and foil the Headmaster's plans.)

Chapters 13 to 16

Read Chapter 13 and invite the children to summarise SPLAT's plan of action (to trap the camera crew's lorries in the quarry, trap the teachers in the swimming pool, lock in the prefects and cut the electric supply to the school). What goes wrong? (They can't stop Eddy from reaching the school and two prefects, Rose and Jeff, are still at large and report back to the Headmaster.) Read on through Chapter 14 and ask: *How does the Headmaster now blackmail Dinah to win the quiz for the school?* (His 'army' of brainwashed children threaten to kill all of SPLAT.) What still remains unanswered about the Headmaster's plan? (What he hopes to achieve when he appears on TV.)

Continue reading the next chapter, pausing after *...school everywhere, with no escape*, to ask the children to explain what is now revealed about the Headmaster's plan. (He intends to rule the world in the same strict, joyless way that he rules the school.) Then read up to where the Headmaster sneezes and encourage the class to explain why a sneeze is such a fitting way to sabotage the Headmaster's speech. (A sneeze is uncontrollable and the Headmaster always wants to be in control.) Complete the story and ask the children to suggest how the author paves the way for a sequel. (The Headmaster promises he will never give up until he has succeeded in ruling the world, and Dinah is now reconciled with the boys and permanently settled in the Hunter family.) Invite the children's initial reactions to the novel.

Subsequent readings

Use subsequent readings to explore the plot structure, key themes and characters in more detail. Before reading the book again, consider what type of story the children think this is – realistic, adventure or mystery? Encourage them to give reasons for their answers.

Plot structure

As they read, invite the children to identify 'hooks' or cliffhangers that make us want to read on. For instance: What is the prick on Dinah's finger at the end of Chapter 3? What is Lloyd's plan at the end of Chapter 12? What will the Headmaster do when he discovers them at the end of Chapter 13? Elicit that the 'hooks' often carry a suggestion of mystery or danger, that sustains pace and excitement in the story. Encourage the children to also identify key plot triggers, for example, Dinah coming to live with the Hunters, Harvey getting caught by a prefect providing the Headmaster with ammunition to blackmail Dinah, and the Eddy Hair Show staging a quiz at the school providing the Headmaster with an opportunity to carry out his plan.

Character

Begin to explore characters in more detail, examining events in order to focus on behaviour and motivation. Dinah, for example, has learned to hide her cleverness but uses it to protect Harvey and foil the Headmaster. Lloyd strongly resents a girl coming into the family and remains suspicious and hostile until Dinah joins forces with SPLAT to triumph over the Headmaster and so wins him over. Younger brother Harvey can be impulsive and curious and often gets into trouble, but he is more friendly towards Dinah, giving her the impetus to help him, but at the same time giving the Headmaster the opportunity to lay a trap for Dinah.

Invite the children to speculate on who, or what, the Headmaster is – demon, alien, robot, or a villainous character who believes (as real-life leaders can, such as Adolf Hitler in the last century) that he is 'meant for greatness' and that his way of rule is for the betterment of the human race. Discuss the theme behind this – the concept of strict order, obedience and submission, against the freedom to think, explore, play and discover.

Setting

Encourage the children to think about the setting – on the surface it's a realistic home and school life, but there are undercurrents of sinister, even deadly goings-on. Discuss the theme of the popular TV show and what it represents – chaos, mess, disorder – the antithesis of the strict order that the Headmaster imposes at school.

Shared reading

SECTION 3

Extract 1

- Read an enlarged copy of Extract 1 with the class.
- Focus on the description of the Headmaster's appearance. Ask the children which words or phrases emphasise his pale, ghostly colouring and circle them. (*Fair, white, colourless as snow, paper-white, pallid, whiteness, ivory-coloured.*) Challenge them to add other words or idioms to the list (such as, wan or white as a sheet).
- Ask: *What clues does Dinah note about his character or behaviour?* (The room is very tidy and empty, his gown is immaculate, he has no time for pleasantries.)
- Can the children pick out any similes or metaphors? (For example, *in heavy folds, like wings, a huge crow, as colourless as snow, eyes... like two black holes.*) What do these comparisons suggest? (A crow is black, menacing and predatory; snow is cold; black holes are mysterious, creepy and unreadable.)
- Elicit that the author uses three methods to create the character: description, action and dialogue. Invite the children to pick out instances of each method, underlining them. For example, (description) *He was tall and thin,* (action) *he went on staring...*, and so on.

Extract 2

- Read the extract and ask the children to explain what is happening and why (Dinah and the boys are being punished for having a snowball fight).
- Can they explain why the boys look at Dinah as if she is an idiot? (They know that the Headmaster can be cruel and callous and he will not care about their welfare, as Dinah expects him to.)
- Ask: *Why might the punishment be dangerous for Harvey?* (He has a weak chest and the cold is affecting his breathing.)
- Highlight the word *cold* and encourage the children to find any other adjectives that emphasise how cold it is (*bluish*). Invite the children to suggest which other parts of speech suggest the bitter cold in this passage (verbs). Challenge them to pick out the verbs (for example, *freezing, shuddered, shivering*).
- Ask them to find any alliterative phrases (*scattering the snow, freezing their fingers, the wind whipped*). What effect do the participle verbs have? (They emphasise that the discomfort is continuous.)

Extract 3

- Read an enlarged copy of Extract 3.
- Explore unfamiliar vocabulary, underlining words and asking the children if they can explain them and/or suggest replacements.
- Encourage the children to explain the impact of the italics and capitals. (The italicised word *pepper* pinpoints Dinah's sudden realisation; the capitals *'A—A—A—TCHOO!'* emphasise the loudness of the sneeze.)
- Re-cap the term onomatopoeia and challenge the children to invent alternative spellings to represent a sneeze.
- Ask: *Which verbs suggest the immense effort required for Dinah to act?* (*Dragging, forced, wrenched, flung.*)
- Consider a sneeze as a poetic punishment for the Headmaster, as a sneeze is something he cannot control, and he must have order and control in everything. Ask: *What tells us he is trying hard to resist?* (His face goes purple and he is pressing his lips together.) Underline the phrase *was forced uncontrollably open* and ask the children to explain why a passive verb is appropriate here.

Extract 1

Chapter 3: The Headmaster

As she stepped through, Dinah glanced quickly round the room. It was the tidiest office she had ever seen. There were no papers, no files, no pictures on the walls. Just a large, empty-topped desk, a filing cabinet, and a bookcase with a neat row of books.

She took it all in in one second and then forgot it as her eyes fell on the man standing by the window. He was tall and thin, dressed in an immaculate black suit. From his shoulders, a long, black teacher's gown hung in heavy folds, like wings, giving him the appearance of a huge crow. Only his head was startlingly white. Fair hair, almost as colourless as snow, lay round a face with paper-white skin and pallid lips. His eyes were hidden behind dark glasses, like two black holes in the middle of all the whiteness.

She cleared her throat. 'Hello. I'm Dinah Glass and I—'

He raised a long, ivory-coloured hand. 'Please do not speak until you are asked. Idle chatter is an inefficient waste of energy.'

Unnervingly, he went on staring at her for a moment or two without saying anything else. Dinah wished she could see the eyes behind the dark lenses. With his eyes hidden, his expression was unreadable.

Extract 2

Chapter 7: The Punishment

For the first ten minutes or so, it was not too bad. The exercise kept them fairly warm. But then the wind started to blow, scattering the snow as they swept it and freezing their fingers.

'I'm so cold,' Harvey said plaintively. 'And we're only halfway across. We'll never get it all swept.'

'Don't give up yet,' Lloyd said grimly. 'This is the easy part. Just you wait until we start on the snowballs.'

Dinah shuddered at the thought, as the wind whipped through her thin school shirt. Then she found that she could not stop shivering. Her whole body was shaking, and her teeth were clattering together uncontrollably. She put down her broom for a moment to clap her arms round herself, for a bit of warmth.

Instantly, from the building behind them, came an irate rapping. Turning, she saw Rose gesturing furiously at her through the window. She picked up her broom again and began to sweep harder, trying to ignore the shaking.

At last the snow was piled into a single heap, almost as tall as Harvey. The three of them laid their brooms down at one side and stared at it.

'I don't think I can do it,' Harvey said woefully. 'My hands are *hurting*.'

Lloyd watched him anxiously. His face had a bluish tinge and he was starting to breathe wheezily.

'Why don't you stop?' Dinah said. 'Tell them you won't do it. I don't suppose the Headmaster would really be angry. He must see—' Then her teeth rattled together so hard that she could not go on speaking.

Lloyd and Harvey said nothing. Just looked at her as though she were completely idiotic and bent down to start making snowballs.

Extract 3

Chapter 16: 'Look into My Eyes'

Millions of cups of tea, in homes everywhere, dropped to the ground unheeded as people slumped forwards in their chairs. In the Hall, the audience nodded and Dinah's eyes began to close. She struggled hard to keep them open, but the lids dropped irresistibly.

Then, just before they finally shut, she saw Harvey leap to his feet. He was pointing straight at her, pointing to the table in front of her. Muzzily, she looked at his lips, trying to see what it was that he was mouthing. If only she did not feel so tired …

Harvey wagged his finger, pointing in a frenzy. And at last she managed to make out what it was he was saying.

'In your hand!'

Funny, she thought sleepily. Why was he interested in her hand? She looked down, forcing her eyes to stay open for a second longer. Oh yes, she thought vaguely. She was still clutching that silly red pepperpot with the black stripes.

' … so, so, *so*, sleepy …'

She gave a huge, exhausted yawn. Pepper? she thought. Then—*pepper*!

That was it! Dragging together all the energy she could muster, she forced herself agonizingly to her feet, wrenched the bottom off the pepperpot and flung the contents, as hard as she could, straight into the Headmaster's face. Then she sank back on to her chair, knowing that she could not do anything more to resist that creeping, soothing voice.

But what had happened to the voice? It has stopped. For a moment there was silence, and she turned her head slowly sideways.

The Headmaster had gone purple in the face, his lips pressed tightly together, his green eyes bulging ludicrously. As she watched, his mouth was forced uncontrollably open in an enormous, a stupendous sneeze.

'A—A—A—TCHOO!'

Plot, character and setting

SECTION 4

Plot drivers

Objective: To understand how writers use different structures to create coherence and impact.
What you need: Copies of *The Demon Headmaster*, whiteboard and photocopiable page 15.

What to do

- Challenge the children to think of five 'plot drivers' (events without which the storyline could not develop) and write their suggestions on the whiteboard. (Suggestions might include: Dinah coming to live with the Hunters, the Headmaster blackmailing Dinah into doing the quiz, the discovery of SPLAT's plan, and so on.)
- Suggest that 'plot drivers' (such as Dinah coming to live with the Hunters) progress the storyline, while other events (for instance, Dinah helping out Lucy in the playground) are used to develop character or setting.
- Hand out photocopiable page 15, inviting the children to explain how each element is involved in the plot and then cut out and re-arrange them in the order they appear in the story.
- When they have finished, bring the class back together and discuss which elements are vital to the plotline and which contribute to character or setting, but do not directly drive the plot forward. (For example, a pepperpot is vital to the plot, while the disused quarry contributes to setting but does not directly drive the plot forward, although it is part of SPLAT's sabotage plans.)

Differentiation
For older/more confident learners: Encourage the children to add one more plot element to the sequence.
For younger/less confident learners: Allow the children to focus on just two or three of the plot elements listed on the photocopiable sheet, such as the pepperpot and maths test.

Mixed emotions

Objective: To understand underlying themes, causes and points of view.
What you need: Copies of *The Demon Headmaster* and photocopiable page 16.
Cross-curricular link: PSHE.

What to do

- Ask the children to summarise how and why Dinah has come to the Demon Headmaster's school. (She has left the Children's Home to be fostered by the Hunters, so she has had to move to a school close to her new home.)
- Discuss what might make things difficult for Dinah – Lloyd resents her arrival, she is the new girl in school, the school seems strange, the prefects and staff are unfriendly.
- Encourage the children to volunteer their own experiences (being sensitive to individual circumstances), such as remembering how they felt starting a new school or difficulties they encountered adjusting to a new family situation (for instance, a new baby or stepfamily).
- Arrange the children into pairs and hand out photocopiable page 16. Explain that they need to think of a situation or event that makes Dinah feel each emotion listed. For example, she feels angry when she finds out the Headmaster knew about their punishment in the snow.

Differentiation
For older/more confident learners: Challenge the children to think of another two emotions Dinah experiences and explain when and why she felt like that.
For younger/less confident learners: Let the children focus on three of Dinah's emotions listed and explain the events or situations in which she felt that way.

The Headmaster

Objective: To explore how writers use language for comic and dramatic effects.
What you need: Copies of *The Demon Headmaster*, whiteboard, individual whiteboards and pens, Extract 1 (page 8).

What to do

- Re-read Extract 1, and remind the children how the author uses description, action and dialogue to create the character of the Headmaster. Write these three headings on the whiteboard.
- Arrange the children into small groups. Assign each group one heading and tell them to scan the novel finding more examples of how the author builds the Headmaster's character with this specific technique. They should note down their findings on their individual whiteboards.
- Allow time for the task to be completed, then bring the class together and invite volunteers to suggest examples to go under their chosen heading. For example: (description) in Chapter 4 we are told *his voice was loud and threatening*; (action) in Chapter 4 we discover that the Headmaster stuck a pin into Dinah's arm; (dialogue) in Chapter 16 he says *'I know I was meant for greatness'*.
- As a class, discuss which examples tell us most about the Headmaster's character.

Differentiation
For older/more confident learners: Assign the children the heading 'dialogue' with which to explore the creation of the character of the Headmaster.
For younger/less confident learners: Ask the children to focus on the 'description' heading, finding at least two examples of how descriptions of the Headmaster develop his character.

Cliffhangers

Objective: To understand how writers use different structures to create coherence and impact.
What you need: Copies of *The Demon Headmaster* and photocopiable page 17.

What to do

- Read together the last section of Chapter 13. Focus on the cliffhanger at the end of the chapter and ask the children to explain what 'hook' the author uses to make us want to read on. (We are left considering what the Headmaster will do to SPLAT.) Invite comparison with cliffhangers at the end of episodes in a TV drama – we are left at a crucial moment, wondering what will happen next.
- Ask the children if they can recall other cliffhangers in the novel and explain what made us want to read on.
- Arrange the children into pairs and hand out photocopiable page 17. Explain that they need to answer the questions left hanging by each cliffhanger, and then cut and paste them into the order they appear in the plot.
- When they have finished, bring the class together and discuss which cliffhangers are the most effective or exciting and how they work by creating suspense.

Differentiation
For older/more confident learners: Challenge the children to identify and add another cliffhanger to the sequence.
For younger/less confident learners: Limit the children to answering three of the cliffhanger questions.

School map

Objective: To sustain engagement with longer texts, using different techniques to make the text come alive.
What you need: Copies of *The Demon Headmaster*, whiteboard, drawing materials.
Cross-curricular link: Geography.

What to do

- Explain to the children that, in this lesson, they are going to focus on the school and its setting in the novel.
- Challenge them to recall any details of rooms or places within the school and its grounds, without referring to the book, and capture their suggestions on the whiteboard. (They may identify the playground, hall, swimming pool, boiler room, prefects' room, cloakroom, Headmaster's office and the disused quarry.)
- Arrange the class into small groups and provide writing and drawing materials or access to individual whiteboards and pens. Ask them to scan the novel looking for any descriptive details about the school and then use the information to draw a simple map of the school and its grounds, labelling the key features.
- Bring the class together and compare each group's school map, inviting feedback.

Differentiation
For older/more confident learners: Ask the children to use the information they have found and utilise their senses to write a descriptive passage, at least one paragraph, about the school premises.
For younger/less confident learners: Invite the children to focus on only two places around the school and provide page numbers to help them locate information.

Where did it happen?

Objective: To make notes on and use evidence from across a text to explain events or ideas.
What you need: Copies of *The Demon Headmaster*, individual whiteboards, pens and maps from the 'School map' lesson.
Cross-curricular link: Geography.

What to do

- Arrange the class into the exact same groups that produced the school maps (in the 'School map' lesson) and ensure they have their maps to refer to.
- Explain that they are now going to annotate their maps with key events that happen in each place, according to the novel. For example, the disused quarry is where the TV camera crew are trapped, while the boiler room is where the Headmaster discovers Harvey taking out the fuses.
- Allow the groups time to scan the novel and make a list of key events. The children should then add these events as labels to their maps, pinpointing the locations where they happened.
- Gather the class together and review their work. The school maps could be used in a class display.

Differentiation
For older/more confident learners: Encourage the children to include as much detail as possible on their maps, without referring to the book.
For younger/less confident learners: Provide the children with a list of key event labels to pinpoint on their maps.

Inspector's report

Objective: To make notes on and use evidence from across a text to explain events or ideas.
What you need: Copies of *The Demon Headmaster* and photocopiable page 18.
Cross-curricular link: PSHE.

What to do

- Invite the children to summarise Dinah's first impressions of her new school. What things tell her that something is amiss? List their suggestions on the whiteboard, such as 'no playing in the playground', and so on.
- Discuss what school inspectors might look for during their visit and note suggestions on the whiteboard (discipline, good teaching, cleanliness, a good atmosphere, academic record, and so on).
- Ask: *Which areas do you think Dinah's school would perform well in and which might give an inspector cause for concern?* For example, the inspector might be impressed with the behaviour of pupils and impressive test results, but be concerned with the punishments used to discipline children and that there is little evidence of artwork.
- Arrange the children into pairs and hand out photocopiable page 18. Explain that they are going to imagine they are a school inspector visiting Dinah's school. Using the novel, they need to note down evidence in the key areas they inspect and make comments about the school for the local authority.
- Give them time to complete the sheet before gathering the class and their findings.

Differentiation
For older/more confident learners: Encourage the children to expand the comments the inspector makes to include his recommendations for creative play, punishment, and so on.
For younger/less confident learners: Let the children concentrate on the first two sections of the inspector's report.

The view

Objective: To develop drama techniques to explore in role a variety of situations and texts or respond to stimuli.
What you need: Copies of *The Demon Headmaster*, whiteboard, individual whiteboards and pens.
Cross-curricular link: Drama.

What to do

- Tell the children they are going to plan and present a trailer for the Eddy Hair Show TV programme.
- Begin by discussing what we know about the show (a fast, zany children's programme which includes sketches, a school quiz, and so on). Capture initial ideas on the whiteboard and encourage the children to cite comparisons with real TV programmes they know and watch.
- Arrange the children into small groups and allow them time to scan the novel to gather more details about the show, its presenter and typical content.
- When they have enough material, they should work together to draft and edit a short trailer for an upcoming edition of the show. Ensure that the children understand the purpose of trailers (to encourage viewers to watch or listen to upcoming programmes on TV or radio).
- Invite volunteers from each group to present their trailers to the class and encourage constructive feedback.

Differentiation
For older/more confident learners: Encourage the children to develop and summarise their own ideas for content, based on what we know about the show.
For younger/less confident learners: Allow the children to base their trailer on the edition of the TV show described in Chapter 12.

Plot drivers

- Explain how each of the following elements feature in the plot, then cut and paste them in the order they appear and identify which are plot drivers.

Snowball fight:
Pepperpot:
Tape recorder:
Disused quarry:
Maths test:

Mixed emotions

- Write down an event or situation that makes Dinah feel each of the following emotions.

Emotion	Event or situation
Awkward	
Lonely	
Angry	
Puzzled	
Excited	

Cliffhangers

- Use your knowledge of the novel to answer these cliffhanger questions, then cut and paste them in the order they appear in the plot.

What will the Headmaster do when he appears on TV?
What is Lloyd's master plan?
What is the strange prick mark on Dinah's finger?
What will the Headmaster do after discovering SPLAT's plan?
How will the prefects punish the children for the snowball fight?

Inspector's report

• Imagine you are a school inspector visiting Dinah's school. Write your observations and comments under the following key areas.

The results of my school inspection

Behaviour of pupils:
Discipline (approach of staff and prefects):
Facilities/activities:
Wall and classroom displays:
Any other comments:

Overall rating (please tick as appropriate):

☐ Excellent ☐ Very good ☐ Acceptable ☐ Needs attention

Talk about it

SECTION 5

Not a girl!

Objective: To understand underlying themes, causes and points of view.
What you need: Copies of *The Demon Headmaster*, individual whiteboards and pens.
Cross-curricular link: PSHE.

What to do

- Read the first section of Chapter 1 and ask the children to explain how Lloyd feels about a girl joining the family (upset, angry, resentful).
- Challenge the children to scan the text, listing all the things Lloyd expects from a girl. (For example, she will put up flower and ballet pictures, be a telltale and goody-goody at school, need looking after, and so on.) Do they think his expectations are fair or are they just stereotypes about girls?
- Arrange the children into pairs and challenge them to draw up a similar list of expectations for a boy entering a family of girls. Ask: *What might the girls dread about the arrival of a boy and how he would behave at home and school?*
- Allow the pairs time to discuss and note their ideas on their whiteboards, then bring the class back together to share ideas.
- Discuss how far any of these stereotypes of girls or boys are fair, and how far they are just prejudices.

Differentiation
For older/more confident learners: Encourage the children to expand both lists, their own and Lloyd's, with more stereotypical ideas about boys and girls.
For younger/less confident learners: Help the children formulate a list of stereotypes about boys by providing prompt categories, such as behaviour, appearance, hobbies or sports.

Prefects

Objective: To use the techniques of dialogic talk to explore ideas, topics or issues.
What you need: Copies of *The Demon Headmaster*, whiteboard, individual whiteboards and pens.
Cross-curricular link: PSHE.

What to do

- Tell the children they are going to focus on the prefects in the novel. Begin by asking them to explain the role of prefects, referring to their own school if relevant. What sort of tasks are prefects expected to do? (Enforce rules, support staff, help run school events, and so on.) Discuss the idea of responsibility and authority, represented by a prefect's badge.
- Ask the children how the prefects in the novel (such as Rose and Jeff) fulfil this role and list their ideas on the whiteboard. (They keep discipline in the playground, enforce punishments and report back to the Headmaster.)
- How would they describe the prefects' characters? (Cold, cruel, bossy, bullying.)
- Arrange the class into small groups to discuss and make notes on the qualities they think a good prefect needs. (For example, well behaved, responsible, confident, kind, friendly and approachable.) Encourage them to also note what a prefect should NOT be. (For example, bossy, a bully, badly behaved, someone who breaks the rules or takes advantage of the role.)
- Bring the class back together and invite groups to share their ideas.

Differentiation
For older/more confident learners: Encourage the children to include discussion of the benefits and drawbacks of being elected a prefect.
For younger/less confident learners: Let the children focus on discussing the characters of Rose and Jeff, directing them to specific sections of the novel.

Hypnotism

Objective: To use exploratory, hypothetical and speculative talk as a tool for clarifying ideas.
What you need: Copies of *The Demon Headmaster*, whiteboard, individual whiteboards and pens.
Cross-curricular links: Science, PSHE.

What to do

- Ask the children what they understand by the term 'hypnotism'. Elicit that it means a relaxed, trance-like state in which someone is susceptible to ideas. Explain that although 'hypnos' means sleep in ancient Greek, the person is actually awake, alert and focussed.
- Challenge them to think how hypnotism is used today and write their suggestions on the whiteboard. (Typically it is used for entertainment shows, to help people overcome problems such as a fear of flying, or to stop addictions such as smoking.) Explain that when hypnotism is used in a therapeutic way it is called 'hypnotherapy'.
- Ask the children to explain how the Headmaster hypnotises (with his voice and eyes). Next, invite them to explain the purpose behind his hypnotism and list their suggestions on the whiteboard. (To force-feed facts, to keep control, to imprint ideas, to manipulate memories, and so on.)
- Discuss how hypnotism used in this way could be a sinister force and why. (It could be used to control people's actions and the way they think.)
- As a class activity, compile a list of the pros and cons of hypnosis.

Differentiation
For older/more confident learners: Encourage speculative thinking, for example: If hypnosis could be used to learn all the facts for an exam, would that be acceptable and, if not, why not?
For younger/less confident learners: Support the children in identifying the Headmaster's purposes by providing prompt questions, such as: What happens in Assembly? Why does Dinah say things mechanically?

SPLAT

Objective: To understand underlying themes, causes and points of view.
What you need: Copies of *The Demon Headmaster* and photocopiable page 22.
Cross-curricular link: History.

What to do

- Explain to the children they are going to focus on the secret society that Dinah joins, known as SPLAT.
- Ask them to explain who has set up SPLAT and why. (The 'Normals' or children who remain beyond the Headmaster's powers, in order to resist and counteract them.) Challenge them to explain why the children might feel the need to set up their own society (because they are outnumbered and want to stay strong and united, to fight for what they believe in). Elicit the word 'resistance' and tell the children that in the Second World War (1939–45) a lot of French people joined the secret 'Resistance', fighting against the Germans who occupied their country. Suggest that SPLAT is a 'resistance' movement.
- Arrange the children into pairs and hand out photocopiable page 22. Invite them to complete the sheet, scanning the novel to find the relevant information.

Differentiation
For older/more confident learners: Encourage the children to suggest more ideas for strategies or activities that SPLAT could employ.
For younger/less confident learners: Provide chapter and page references to help the children locate relevant information about SPLAT (see Chapter 10).

Talk about it

SECTION 5

School timetables

Objective: To infer writers' perspectives from what is written and from what is implied.
What you need: Copies of *The Demon Headmaster*, whiteboard and photocopiable page 23.
Cross-curricular link: PSHE.

What to do

- Challenge the children to summarise the type of things they would learn at the Headmaster's school and capture their suggestions on the whiteboard. (For instance, the names of capital cities, multiplication sums, facts about the solar system, and so on.)
- Arrange the class into pairs and hand out photocopiable page 23. Explain that they are going to fill in a lesson timetable for the school. For example, in history the children might be taught the dates when all the monarchs ruled England; in geography they might be taught the names of different countries and their capital cities.
- Bring the class back together and share ideas for the timetable.
- Ask: *What do you think the author's view of this type of education is and why?* (She thinks it is dull, rote-learning; she describes the children as robots as they are having facts and figures pumped into them, not learning to think for themselves.)

Differentiation
For older/more confident learners: Encourage the children to complete an alternative timetable, containing a list of lesson activities the Demon Headmaster would never allow.
For younger/less confident learners: Allow the children to focus on three lessons on the timetable, referring to the novel to help them.

Eddy and the Head

Objective: To improvise using a range of drama strategies and conventions to explore themes such as hopes, fears and desires.
What you need: Copies of *The Demon Headmaster* and photocopiable page 24.
Cross-curricular link: Drama.

What to do

- Explain to the children that they are going to dramatise a 'question time' session, with the Headmaster and Eddy Hair in the hot-seat, giving their views on school-related topics.
- Begin by discussing how the Headmaster and Eddy Hair are 'opposites' in character. (The Headmaster is strict, controlling and hates mess, while Eddy loves mess, chaos and surprises.)
- Ask for volunteers to play the roles of Eddy, the Headmaster and a chairman (who will take questions from the groups). In preparation for their roles, encourage them to gather information on both characters' personalities and views.
- Arrange the rest of the class into small groups and allow them time to think up questions on school-related topics (such as, views on school uniforms, discipline in school, school rules, playground activities, and so on).
- Begin the drama session with the chairman inviting each group to ask questions in turn to both Eddy and the Headmaster.
- When the drama session has finished, hand out photocopiable page 24 and tell the children to work individually to complete it.

Differentiation
For older/more confident learners: Encourage the children to add two further topics with accompanying speech for each character to their sheet.
For younger/less confident learners: Invite the children to focus on either one or two school-related topics from the recommended list provided.

SPLAT

- Complete the following information about SPLAT.

Chairman:

Members:

Meeting place:

Motto (entry code):

What is the Register of Rules?:

List three things SPLAT members do:

1 ______________________________

2 ______________________________

3 ______________________________

School timetable

- Create a timetable for the Demon Headmaster's school, summarising the lesson content.

For example:

Time	Subject	Lesson content
9.00–11.00	Geography	Learn and recite names of capital cities

Time	Subject	Lesson content
	English	
	Maths	
	Geography	
	History	
	Science	
	PE	

Eddy and the Head

• Choose three school-related topics and write down what the Headmaster and Eddy Hair might say about each of them.

1. Topic: ______________________

Headmaster:

Eddy Hair:

2. Topic: ______________________

Headmaster:

Eddy Hair:

3. Topic: ______________________

Headmaster:

Eddy Hair:

Possible topics:

school uniforms prefects the importance of play time
favourite school motto discipline school rules

Get writing

SECTION 6

Dinah's diary

Objective: To vary the pace and develop the viewpoint through the use of direct and reported speech, portrayal of action and selection of detail.
What you need: Copies of *The Demon Headmaster*, whiteboard, individual whiteboards and pens.

What to do

- Inform the children that, in this lesson, they will be drafting a diary entry that Dinah might write after her first day at her new school.
- Discuss the key events and experiences that Dinah could record in her diary about when she first arrives at the Hunters and starts her new school. Encourage them to consider: what she thinks about the Hunter home; her first impressions of Mrs Hunter, Lloyd and Harvey; what she notices walking to school; and her encounter with the Headmaster. Capture suggestions on the whiteboard.
- Invite the children to think about how Dinah is feeling, again noting down suggestions. (Possibly she feels a bit lonely, awkward about moving in with a new family, puzzled by her first impressions of the school, the Head and pupils.)
- Revise the key features of diaries (they are written in the first person, they can be informal, even note-style in form, chronological recounts).
- Allow the children time to re-read and scan the first three chapters, then draft and edit Dinah's diary entry.
- Invite volunteers to read out their diary entry and encourage constructive feedback.

Differentiation
For older/more confident learners: Ask the children to write another diary entry by Dinah, for the day of the snowball fight.
For younger/less confident learners: Scan the first three chapters as a shared activity, noting down for the children the key events or impressions that Dinah might record.

Colourful words

Objective: To explore how writers use language for comic and dramatic effects.
What you need: Copies of *The Demon Headmaster*, whiteboard and photocopiable page 28.

What to do

- Focus on the character of Lloyd and challenge the children to summarise what we know about him (he has a mop of wild hair, is chairman of SPLAT, is Harvey's older brother and keeps him out of trouble at school, and so on). How would they describe his character? (Bold, outspoken, excitable.)
- Focus on the language Lloyd uses when he is angry or excited about something, challenging the children to suggest parodies of his exclamations (such as, 'pink bananas' or 'bright green ginger nuts'). Capture some of the best suggestions on the whiteboard.
- Hand out photocopiable page 28 and tell the children to complete it. Explain that they need to add the missing words in Lloyd's exclamations and then think of their own.
- When they have finished, bring the class together and invite volunteers to share their own Lloyd-style exclamations. Encourage feedback and praise their efforts.

Differentiation
For older/more confident learners: Encourage the children to compose their own Lloyd-style exclamations without using the word bank.
For younger/less confident learners: Let the children create just one of their own Lloyd-style exclamations.

Head poem

Objective: To adapt non-narrative forms and styles to write fiction or factual texts, including poems.
What you need: Copies of *The Demon Headmaster*, whiteboard, individual whiteboards and pens, Extract 1 (page 8).

What to do

- Inform the children that they will be writing a poem about the Demon Headmaster. Begin by mind-mapping words to describe him (mysterious, creepy, sinister, threatening).
- Re-read Extract 1 and ask the children to scan the text for key descriptive words and phrases, capturing them on the whiteboard (*a huge crow, colourless as snow, paper-white skin*, and so on).
- Arrange the children into pairs and tell them to scan the novel for more key words and phrases describing the Headmaster's appearance, voice or manner, noting them on their own whiteboards. Encourage them to use the words they find to form their own epithets (such as green-eyed, crow-like, pallid-lipped, snowy-haired).
- When they have finished, ask the pairs to share their ideas and write key words or phrases on the whiteboard. Invite the children to develop the words and epithets into similes or metaphors (for example, *black as a crow, pools of green*).
- Challenge the children to use the words and phrases to write a short descriptive poem about the Headmaster.
- When they have finished, invite volunteers to share their poems, encouraging feedback.

Differentiation
For older/more confident learners: Challenge the children to compose a haiku poem (5-7-5 syllable form).
For younger/less confident learners: Help the children by modelling some lines such as: A stooping figure / Black as a crow / Wings furled / Eyes fixed.

Eddy Hair's profile page

Objective: To independently write and present a text with the reader and purpose in mind.
What you need: Copies of *The Demon Headmaster* and photocopiable page 29.
Cross-curricular link: ICT.

What to do

- Explain to the children that they are to plan and write a profile of the TV presenter Eddy Hair for a social networking site.
- Arrange the children into pairs and ask them to scan the novel to find out as many relevant facts about Eddy as they can. Encourage them also to use their imagination to add information or ideas about Eddy's pastimes, interests, favourite music, and so on.
- When the children have gathered enough information, hand out photocopiable page 29 and invite them to use the information to complete the sheet.
- After completing the sheet, challenge the children to work independently to create a profile of Eddy, using their ICT skills.

Differentiation
For older/more confident learners: Invite the children to use their imagination to add extra sections to their profile page, such as favourite TV shows, quotations, hobbies, books, and so on.
For younger/less confident learners: Let the children focus on the first four sections of the profile page and/or provide page references to help them locate relevant information.

Register of Rules

Objective: In non-narrative, establish, balance and maintain viewpoints.
What you need: Copies of *The Demon Headmaster*, individual whiteboards and pens.
Cross-curricular links: PSHE, citizenship.

What to do

- Ask the children to explain what the 'Register of Rules' is in the novel. (A book in which the members of SPLAT keep all the new rules the Headmaster makes, so that they can swap details and avoid getting caught out by them.)
- Challenge them to suggest one or two rules that might be listed (such as no playing anywhere in the school grounds or everyone must wear the official school uniform).
- Arrange the children into pairs and tell them to scan the novel to find evidence of any other rules, noting them on their whiteboards.
- Invite them to add other rules that they think the Headmaster might introduce (for example, no art and craft work that could cause mess, no noise when playing sports, no food to be eaten anywhere other than the dining hall, and so on).
- Allow the pairs time to draft their Register of Rules, then invite them to share ideas with the class.
- Discuss which rules seem fair (if any) and compare them with the children's own school rules. Which rules do they think are fair and/or sensible and which would they get rid of and why?

Differentiation
For older/more confident learners: Challenge the children to draw up their own list of fair school rules.
For younger/less confident learners: Help the children identify the school rules by providing chapter and/or page references.

Sabotage!

Objective: To make notes on and use evidence from across a text to explain events or ideas.
What you need: Copies of *The Demon Headmaster*, individual whiteboards, pens and photocopiable page 30.

What to do

- Challenge the children to explain the 'climax' of the plot and the main cliffhanger. (Can SPLAT stop the Great School Quiz from taking place and so prevent the Headmaster's plan to hypnotise millions of TV viewers?)
- Arrange them into pairs and hand out photocopiable page 30. Explain that they are required to write instructions for each member of SPLAT to carry out Lloyd's plan to sabotage the Eddy Hair Show. Briefly revise verb forms for instructions before they begin (imperatives or second person verbs).
- Advise the pairs to scan Chapter 13 and make notes on their whiteboards, before completing the sheet.
- When they have finished, discuss which parts of the plan work well and which fail and why. (For example, the teachers are successfully trapped in the swimming pool, but Eddy Hair gets past Ian and Rose and Jeff remain at large.)

Differentiation
For older/more confident learners: Challenge the children to devise another sabotage plan which could have successfully foiled the Headmaster's plan to appear on TV.
For younger/less confident learners: Allow the children to focus on completing the instructions for three of the members of SPLAT.

Colourful words

- Complete the missing words in Lloyd's exclamations below.

1. Purple ______________________________
2. ______________________________ sausages
3. Rubber ______________________________
4. Orange ______________ with ______________ skins
5. ______________________________ sandwiches

- Now invent your own Lloyd-style exclamations using the word bank below as well as your own ideas.

______________________ ______________________

______________________ ______________________

______________________ ______________________

______________________ ______________________

______________________ ______________________

______________________ ______________________

______________________ ______________________

______________________ ______________________

Word bank

carrots	pasta	turnips	pomegranates
bright pink	crimson	pea-green	turquoise

Eddy Hair's profile page

- Imagine you are Eddy Hair and complete each of the fields below to create your social networking profile.

Name:

Profile picture:

About me:

What I do:

My catchphrase:

What I drive:

Three of my favourite things:

Three things I want to do before I die:

Sabotage!

- Write instructions for each member of SPLAT to carry out Lloyd's sabotage plan.

Harvey:

Lloyd:

Ian:

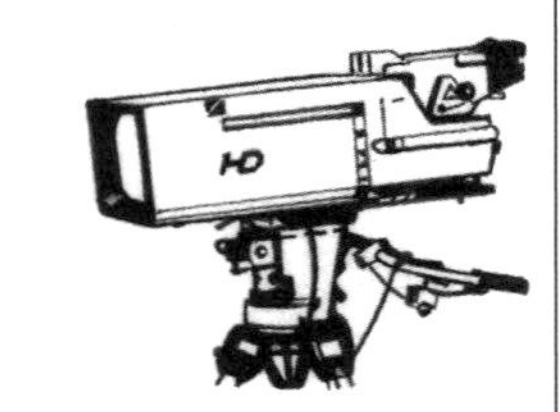

Dinah:

Mandy:

Ingrid:

Assessment

SECTION 7

Assessment advice

Gillian Cross' story combines familiar elements of children's novels (a school setting, a group of peers working together to outwit a villainous enemy and a clever, sympathetic heroine) with some darker, and more mysterious elements reminiscent of science fiction or thriller mysteries. The boy-girl dynamic and purple-haired Eddy Hair provide humour and light relief against the darker and more sinister episodes in which Dinah is hypnotised against her will or finds herself speaking or writing mechanically. Most disturbing of all is the episode when she and her fellow members of SPLAT are threatened by the robotic figures of the hypnotised children, intent on killing them like straw dolls.

Read & Respond encourages children to carry out a range of activities to exercise their speaking, listening, reading and writing skills. Assessment should be an ongoing process, recording progress and highlighting areas that need improvement. It should be based on contributions in shared class work as well as on written individual or group work. Begin each lesson by explaining the learning objective and, where possible, relate it to other literacy and cross-curricular work. At the end of each lesson, encourage the children to assess their own work against the objectives set and to decide which areas need further practice. They should also be encouraged to provide constructive feedback for writing partners and groups.

Children can create their own assessment activities. For example, they could use photocopiable page 32 to develop a multiple choice quiz, by devising further incomplete statements about the story with three possible answers to complete them, one true and two false. For example:

The headmaster wears dark glasses...

because he cannot stand the light.
in order to hide his hypnotic eyes.
because he has poor eyesight.

The children could also devise spelling tests based on parts of speech (verbs, nouns, adjectives, adverbs) and compile lists of similes and metaphors. For photocopiable page 32, they are required to complete statements about the novel and this could be used as a comprehension assessment.

The Great Book Quiz

Objective: To read between the lines and find evidence for their interpretation.
What you need: Photocopiable page 32.

What to do

- As a class, discuss if the children enjoyed *The Demon Headmaster* and, if so, why.
- Ask: *What sort of story do you think it is?* (Adventure, mystery, thriller?) Encourage them to give reasons for their answers.
- Invite the children to nominate their favourite parts or aspects of the story and, again, explain their reasons.
- Challenge them to identify the writer's main themes in the story. (For example, the importance of freedom and learning to think for yourself; the danger of an egotistical and powerful ruler.) They should cite evidence for their suggestions.
- Hand out photocopiable page 32 and explain that they are required to complete the quiz-style statements using their knowledge of the novel. Let the children work on their own to complete the photocopiable sheet.
- When the children have finished, they should work with a writing partner and each devise more incomplete statements about the novel for their writing partner then to complete.

The Great Book Quiz

- Complete these unfinished statements about the novel.

The Headmaster wears dark glasses to…

___

___

The Register of Rules is…

___

___

Dinah feels like Winston Smith when…

___

___

Harvey is punished with the maths test for…

___

___

The Headmaster blackmails Dinah into doing the quiz by…

___

___

The Headmaster cannot finish his broadcast because…

___

___